Safety

WAYLAND

First published in 2008
by Wayland

Copyright © Wayland 2008

Wayland
338 Euston Road
London NW1 3BH

Wayland Australia
Level 17/207 Kent Street
Sydney, NSW 2000

All rights reserved
Senior Editor: Jennifer Schofield
Designer: Sophie Pelham
Digital colour: Carl Gordon

CIP data:
 Gogerly, Liz
   Safety. - (Looking after me)
   1. Accidents - Prevention - Juvenile literature
   2. Offenses against the person - Prevention -
Juvenile literature
   3. Safety education - Juvenile literature
   I. Title
   613.6

ISBN: 978 0 7502 5306 2
Printed in China

Wayland is a division of Hachette Children's Books,
an Hachette Livre UK company.

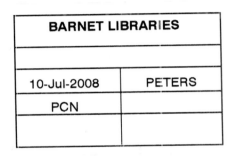

Looking After Me

Safety

Written by Liz Gogerly
Illustrated by Mike Gordon

WAYLAND

Going to the park was my idea of fun.

Dad said it was his idea of a nightmare.

Molly!
Sunblock and hat!

5

The troubles usually began on the way to the park. I wanted to get there VERY quickly.

I never bothered to STOP, LOOK and LISTEN when I crossed the road.

As soon as we got
to the park, I was off.
Sometimes, I pretended to be

a dare-devil pilot...

Until I landed in dog muck.

Another time
I pretended

I was a champion
ice-skater.

10

I whizzed around and around, but my poor dog fell in the ice. I didn't skate again!

I pretended to be a world-famous mountain climber, too. The other kid was OK but I got a bump on my head.

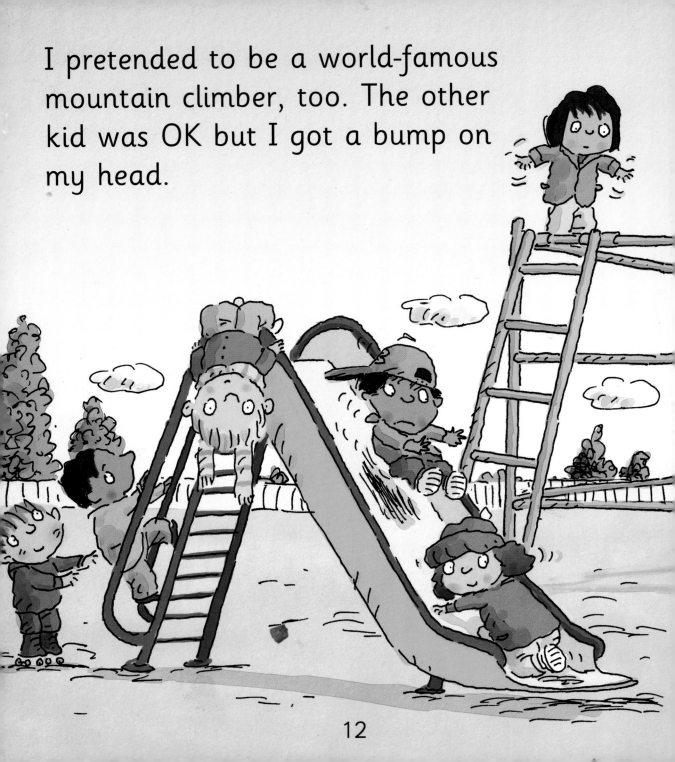

I didn't climb up the slide the wrong way again.

13

Dad always said he didn't know what was going to happen next when we were at the park.

Don't pick up sharp things, Molly!

He said there was always an accident just waiting to happen.

He told me it was dangerous
to go up to strangers' dogs,
but I never listened to him.

Then, a dog got angry
with me.

I didn't touch strange
dogs again.

One day, I really wished I'd listened to my Dad. He always told me to stay where he could see me, and I could see him.

He also told me to be careful of strangers.

At first, the man outside the shop seemed friendly.

But then I got a funny feeling...
I thought he was lying.

I shouted loudly, but nobody came.

So, I pretended I was an Olympic runner. I ran and ran and ran.

I was lucky.

The man wasn't behind me.
But I was lost.

Dad told me that if I was ever lost, I should find a grown-up with other kids, or a police officer, but I couldn't see anyone I trusted.

Dad also said I could ask for help
in a shop, a library or another place
I already knew.

Luckily, I remembered my address and telephone number.

And very soon, Mum and Dad came to fetch me.

Now I listen to my parents and I try to keep safe.

I also tell my mum and dad where I'm going.

I'm going to the moon.

But I still have lots of adventures.

NOTES FOR PARENTS AND TEACHERS

SUGGESTIONS FOR READING **LOOKING AFTER ME: SAFETY** WITH CHILDREN

Safety is the story of an energetic and adventurous young girl called Molly. At the start of the book, we read about Molly in a variety of situations that could be dangerous. She is in such a rush to get to the park that she forgets the basic rules of road safety. This would be a good opportunity to ask the children about what they know about road safety. Afterwards, you could talk to them about how they should behave when there is traffic. Another point worth raising is remembering to slow down and think about what you are doing, whatever the situation may be.

Molly's trip to the park is filled with safety issues for children. Trees, frozen ponds, playground rides and dogs all threaten children's safety. Let the children talk about these everyday hazards. Perhaps there are other safety issues that have not been covered in this story that they have experienced. In the section where Molly discovers 'treasure', which is actually broken glass, you could broaden the discussion to include other sharp objects, such as discarded needles or dangerous objects in the house.

One of the most important things we can teach children is what to do if they encounter a stranger. Molly has a gut reaction about the man in the park. Children often know when something or someone feels strange and it's important that they act on those feelings. Molly listens to her own feelings and makes her escape. Talk about this situation with the children and discuss what they would and should do in a similar situation. In this story, Molly also has to cope with being lost. Fortunately, she did listen to her father's advice and followed his instructions. This is an opportunity to find out how the children would react in a similar situation. It is also a good time to urge the children to learn their full name, address and telephone number in case of an emergency.

LOOKING AFTER ME AND THE NATIONAL CURRICULUM

The Looking After Me series of books is aimed at children studying PSHE at Key Stage 1. In the section *Knowledge, Skills and Understanding: Developing a Healthy, Safer Lifestyle* of the National Curriculum, it is stated that pupils are expected to 'learn about themselves as developing individuals and as members of their communities, building on their own experiences and on the early learning goals for personal, social and emotional development.' Children are expected to learn:
• how to make simple choices that improve their health and well-being to maintain personal hygiene;
• how some diseases spread and can be controlled;
• about the process of growing from young to old and how people's needs change;
• the names of the main parts of the body;
• that all household products, including medicines, can be harmful if not used properly;
• rules for, and ways of, keeping safe, including basic road safety, and about people who can help them to stay safe.

BOOKS TO READ

Look Out on the Road Claire Llewellyn
(Wayland, 2006)

Once Upon a Dragon: Stranger Safety for Kids (and Dragons) Jean E. Pendziwol
(Kids Can Press, 2006)

I Can be Safe: A First Look at Safety Pat Thomas (Wayland, 2004)

ACTIVITY

Ask the children to identify methods of making the area around their school or home safe. For example, cycleways, pavements, fencing, no parking zones, road signs, pedestrian crossings. Do they think each of these methods is important? Do they work? How could they make the areas safer?

INDEX